Perfect Pressure Cooking

With Debra Murray

Acknowledgements

This cookbook took the efforts of many talented people, without them, I would not have been able to make this book a reality.

First, I would like to thank my husband Martin and my daughter Nevar. They inspired me to create these wonderful recipes. I want to thank my parents and my sister Gail for such a wonderful childhood, they are the best friends in the world.

My sincere gratitude to Chef Wolfgang Puck, I cannot thank you enough for this wonderful career and letting me share the set with you. Thank you for the laughter, I adore you as a chef and a person. I continue to be amazed and inspired by you.

A special thanks to Jonathan Schwartz for making these books. I want to thank Sydney Silverman and Mike Sanseverino, they are the nicest people one could work for.

I want to thank all the incredible HSN viewers who have embraced my books. Your support has been overwhelming and for that I am ever grateful.

I am so lucky to have a remarkable book staff. Daniel Koren for being so patient and having such incredible skills to make these books so amazing. Christina Chancey, for your brilliant food styling and recipe testing. Chris Davis and his assistant Erica for the food photography as well as Nevar Murray and Tracy Ferguson for their art direction. I would be remiss if I did not thank Marian Getz for all the wonderful things she teaches me as well as my makeup artists Julie and Ginny.

Introduction

The pressure cooker is surrounded by stories ranging from lids flying to dripping soup from the ceiling. While older pressure cookers may have caused these episodes, today's generation of pressure cookers are modified to ensure safe and easy cooking. This appliance is designed to use steam pressure to break down the fibers of the food allowing for faster cooking times. Tough meats become tender quickly, vegetables and grains are infused with flavors, and foods retain their nutrients. Although the pressure cooker is mainly used as a timesaving device, it works for fine cooking as well.

Debra Murray has been my assistant at the Home Shopping Network for ten years, and I know her passion for quality appliances that can make anyone a better cook. Debra knows how to use the pressure cooker in remarkable ways. Her passion for cooking and experimental nature created this amazing collection of recipes. I have urged her to share them with as many people as possible through this book.

An extremely talented cook, Debra shares my WELL (Wolfgang's Eat, Love, Live!™) philosophy of good cooking and warm hospitality. I believe everyone should use the freshest, all-natural ingredients, locally grown, organic when possible, and raised using sustainable humane methods.

I learned long ago, beside my mother and grandmother, one should always put lots of love into cooking. This is evident in this book of Debra Murray's pressure cooker recipes.

Table Of Contents

Soups, Stews & Stocks
Page 8

Vegetables
Page 38

Rice, Beans & Pastas
Page 60

Table Of Contents

Pressure Cooking Tips

Here is a list of tips to help you get the most from your pressure cooker:

- It is very important to have a liquid such as water, stock, juice or wine in the pressure cooker in order to create steam. Thicker liquids such as barbecue or tomato sauce will not create steam. At least 1 to 2 cups of liquid are necessary to create adequate steam.

- Each function has its own specific temperature and pressure. A suggested function may seem odd to you but I chose it because it achieved the best results. When converting these recipes for pressure cookers other than the Wolfgang Puck pressure cooker, use your high pressure function whenever you see the MEAT function and your low pressure function whenever you see the VEGGIE function.

- When cooking a rice, bean or pasta dish, do not fill the pressure cooker more than halfway. When cooking soups or stocks, do not exceed the ⅔ mark.

- If you live in higher altitudes, you may increase the cooking times slightly. I suggest adding 5% cooking time for every 1000 feet above sea level.

- All of the recipes were tested by weight so if you wish to cook a larger piece of meat, you will need to increase the cooking time. Add 10 minutes to the suggested cooking time for every additional pound of meat.

- If your meat is not as tender as you would like, simply add ½ cup of liquid and increase the cooking time by 10 minutes. Meat is not graded or marbled with the same amount of fat, so there may be some fluctuation in cooking times.

- These are some guidelines for rice that work for me: On the RICE function, white rice cooks in 6 minutes, brown and wild rice in 20 minutes.

- You should carefully wash the lid and remove the regulator for cleaning. The valves and regulator need to be clean for the pressure cooker to function properly. The gasket should always be hand washed and properly fitted back on the lid as it prevents the steam from escaping. If not properly installed, steam will escape under the lid and pressure will not be achieved.

- I do not recommend using the quick release method for letting the pressure out. I have timed the recipes in this book with the pressure going out on its own. Using the quick release method may affect your results. Also, remember to never attempt to open the lid while pressure cooking is in progress.

I have also included a pressure cooker cooking chart for your reference:

INGREDIENT	AMOUNT	FUNCTION	TIME (Minutes)	LIQUID SUGGESTED (Cups)
VEGETABLES				
Artichokes, trimmed	3 med	Veggie	14	2
Beans, Black	1 cup	Veggie	12	2
Beans, Navy	1 cup	Veggie	8	2 - 2 1/2
Beans, Pinto	1 cup	Rice	15	3
Beans, Red Kidney	1 cup	Rice	20	3 1/2
Beans, String	1 lb	Veggie	3	1
Beets	6 med	Veggie	15	2
Cabbage head, quartered	1 med	Veggie	10	2
Carrots 2" pieces	2 cups	Veggie	5	1
Corn on the cob	6 ears	Veggie	4	1 1/2
Parsnips, cubed	2 cups	Veggie	4	1 1/2
Squash , Acorn, halved	4 halves	Veggie	13	2
Squash, Butternut, 1/2" slices	8 slices	Veggie	4	1 1/2
MEATS, POULTRY, SEAFOOD				
Beef Brisket	3 lbs	Meat	90	2-3
Beef Ribs	6 whole	Meat	30	2
Chicken, boneless, skinless pieces, frozen	4 lbs	Meat	5	2
Chicken, legs	4 whole	Meat	20	2
Chicken, quartered	1 whole	Meat	20	2
Chicken, whole	3 lbs	Meat	20	3
Chuck Roast	3 lbs	Meat	75	2-3
Corned Beef	3 lbs	Meat	90	3
Baby Back Ribs	2 slabs	Meat	20	2
Lamb Shanks	2-3 lbs	Meat	30	2
Pork Chops (8-10 oz each)	3-4	Meat	12	2
Pork Loin	2 lbs	Meat	22	3
Short Ribs	3 lbs	Meat	35	2
Spare Ribs	1 slab	Meat	30	2
Stew Meat 1" pieces	3 lbs	Meat	18	4
Turkey Breast	5 lbs	Meat	45	3
Veal Shanks (8 oz each)	3	Meat	30	2
POTATOES				
Potato, Baking	4 large	Veggie	15	2
Potatoes, Red Bliss (2 oz each)	up to 20	Veggie	7	2
Potatoes, White, cubed	3 cups	Veggie	5	1 1/2

Soups
Stews &
Stocks

Function

Time   Delay Time

Keep Warm   Cancel

Butternut Squash Soup

Ingredients:

6 cups butternut squash, peeled and diced

3 cups chicken stock

1 cup apple cider

2 medium apples, peeled and seeded

2 teaspoons curry powder

1 medium onion, diced

½ teaspoon salt

1. Place all ingredients into pressure cooker; secure lid.
2. Set pressure cooker to SOUP and timer to 10 minutes.
3. When cooking is complete, puree the soup in a blender and serve.

Deb's Tip:
For a different flavor, try using jerk spice instead of curry.

15 Bean Soup

Ingredients:

1 pound 15 bean soup mix

1 large onion, diced

1 can (28 ounces) crushed tomatoes

3 celery stalks, chopped

1 ham hock

1 pound pork shoulder, diced into 1-inch cubes

2 garlic cloves, minced

1 tablespoon parsley

1 teaspoon rosemary

2 teaspoons salt

1 teaspoon black pepper

8 cups chicken stock

1. Place all ingredients into pressure cooker; secure lid.

2. Set pressure cooker to SOUP and timer to 30 minutes.

3. When cooking is complete, remove ham hock and serve.

French Onion Soup

Ingredients:

4 large sweet onions, sliced

2 cups beef stock

1 tablespoon balsamic vinegar

¼ cup red wine

2 sprigs thyme

1 bay leaf

½ teaspoon salt

½ teaspoon freshly ground pepper

8 ounces Gruyere cheese, sliced

1. Place all ingredients, except cheese, into pressure cooker; secure lid.
2. Set pressure cooker to SOUP and timer to 20 minutes.
3. When cooking is complete, remove thyme and bay leaf.
4. Turn oven to broil.
5. Ladle soup into oven safe bowls and top each bowl with 2 slices of cheese.
6. Place bowls under broiler for 2 minutes or until cheese is melted.
7. Serve immediately.

Tomato Soup

Ingredients:

4 pounds ripe tomatoes

2 cups chicken stock

2 sprigs thyme

1 small onion, quartered

2 large carrots, peeled

3 celery stalks

1 small potato, peeled and halved

2 teaspoons salt

1 teaspoon freshly ground pepper

2 tablespoons butter

1. Place tomatoes, stock and thyme into pressure cooker; secure lid.
2. Set pressure cooker to SOUP and timer to 20 minutes.
3. When cooking is complete, remove thyme and press tomatoes through a sieve to remove seeds and skin.
4. Add strained tomato liquid and remaining ingredients, except butter, to pressure cooker; secure lid.
5. Set pressure cooker to SOUP and timer to 10 minutes.
6. When cooking is complete, transfer soup to a blender.
7. Add butter to blender and puree until desired consistency.

Deb's Tip:
Serve this soup with a grilled cheese sandwich.

14

Chicken Soup

Ingredients:

1 whole chicken

1 sprig rosemary

1 sprig thyme

1 medium onion, quartered

6 cups water

1 tablespoon kosher salt

6 whole peppercorns

2 celery stalks, sliced

2 carrots, peeled and sliced

1 parsnip, peeled and sliced

1 tablespoon fresh parsley, chopped

1. Place chicken, rosemary, thyme, onions, water, salt and peppercorns into pressure cooker; secure lid.
2. Set pressure cooker to MEAT and timer to 45 minutes.
3. When cooking is complete, strain the stock; set aside.
4. Remove chicken meat from bones and place meat back into the pressure cooker.
5. Add strained stock, celery, carrots and parsnips to pressure cooker; secure lid.
6. Set pressure cooker to SOUP and timer to 5 minutes.
7. When cooking is complete, sprinkle soup with parsley and serve.

Ginger Carrot Soup

Makes 4 to 6 servings

Ingredients:

6 large carrots, peeled and chopped

1 medium onion, diced

2 tablespoons fresh ginger, minced

2 cups chicken stock

½ cup orange juice

1 teaspoon salt

½ teaspoon freshly ground pepper

1. Place all ingredients into pressure cooker; secure lid.
2. Set pressure cooker to SOUP and timer to 5 minutes.
3. When cooking is complete, puree soup in a blender and serve.

Beef Bourguignon

Makes 4 to 6 servings

Ingredients:

1 tablespoon flour

1 teaspoon salt

½ teaspoon freshly ground pepper

1½ pounds beef sirloin, cut into 1-inch pieces

2 garlic cloves, minced

1 cup burgundy wine

1½ cups beef stock

1 tablespoon tomato paste

1 sprig thyme

1 cup frozen pearl onions

1 cup small mushrooms

3 large carrots, peeled and sliced diagonally into 2-inch pieces

3 parsnips, peeled and cut into 2-inch pieces

1. In a bowl, combine flour, salt and pepper; mix well.
2. Roll beef pieces in flour mixture; shake off excess.
3. Place beef and remaining ingredients into pressure cooker; secure lid.
4. Set pressure cooker to STEW and timer to 20 minutes.
5. When cooking is complete, serve immediately.

Beef Stew

Makes 6 to 8 servings

Ingredients:

2 pounds stew beef, cut into 1-inch cubes

1 cup beef stock

1 medium onion, diced

2 sprigs thyme

1 teaspoon salt

½ teaspoon black pepper

1 pound small red potatoes, peeled and quartered

2 celery stalks, cut into 1-inch pieces

1 package (1 pound) baby carrots

1 can (14½ ounces) diced tomatoes

1 can (10¾ ounces) golden mushroom soup

1. Add beef, stock, onions, thyme, salt and pepper to pressure cooker; secure lid.
2. Set pressure cooker to STEW and timer to 20 minutes.
3. When cooking is complete, add potatoes, celery, carrots and tomatoes to pressure cooker; secure lid.
4. Set pressure cooker to VEGGIE and timer to 5 minutes.
5. When cooking is complete, remove thyme and stir in mushroom soup; let heat and serve.

Deb's Tip:
Serve with crusty French bread.

Mediterranean Turkey Meatball Soup

Makes 6 to 8 servings

Meatballs:

1 pound ground turkey breast

½ cup mushrooms, diced

1 small onion, minced

½ cup Italian breadcrumbs with Romano cheese

1 teaspoon garlic salt

1 large egg, beaten

Soup:

4 cups chicken stock

½ cup carrots, peeled and sliced into ½-inch pieces

2 celery stalks, thinly sliced

1 small onion, diced

1 bay leaf

1 can (14½ ounces) diced tomatoes

1 can (19 ounces) northern white beans

1 cup dry pasta

1 teaspoon garlic salt

1. In a bowl, combine meatball ingredients; mix well.
2. Form meat mixture into 1-inch meatballs.
3. Place meatballs and soup ingredients into pressure cooker; secure lid.
4. Set pressure cooker to SOUP and timer to 15 minutes.
5. When cooking is complete, remove bay leaf and serve.

Deb's Tip:
Add a touch of fresh pesto to this soup.

Split Pea Soup

Ingredients:

1 package (16 ounces) split peas with seasoning packet

2 cups pork shoulder, diced

3 carrots, peeled and sliced

½ cup onions, diced

2 celery stalks, sliced

2 garlic cloves, minced

1 bay leaf

2 tablespoons fresh parsley, chopped

1 tablespoon salt

½ teaspoon freshly ground pepper

1 teaspoon vinegar

6 cups water

1. Place all ingredients into pressure cooker; secure lid.
2. Set pressure cooker to SOUP and timer to 10 minutes.
3. When cooking is complete, remove bay leaf and serve.

Low Calorie White Chili

Makes 4 to 6 servings

Ingredients:

2 pounds ground turkey breast, crumbled

1½ cups chicken stock

1 envelope chili seasoning for white chili

1 medium onion, diced

2 garlic cloves, minced

1 green chile, seeds and membrane removed, diced

1 tablespoon fresh cilantro, chopped

2 cans (15½ ounces each) white kidney beans, drained

2 cans (10¾ ounces each) tomatoes with green chiles and lime

½ cup Monterey Jack cheese, shredded

1. Place all ingredients, except cheese, into pressure cooker; secure lid.
2. Set pressure cooker to STEW and timer to 20 minutes.
3. When cooking is complete, add cheese, stir and serve.

Deb's Tip:
For some extra texture, try adding a cup of corn to this chili.

Texas Style Chili

Ingredients:

2 pound beef sirloin, cut into 1-inch pieces

1 pound pork loin, cut into 1-inch pieces

1 bell pepper, diced

1 medium onion, diced

3 garlic cloves, minced

1 envelope chili seasoning

1 teaspoon cumin

1 teaspoon salt

½ teaspoon freshly ground pepper

2 cups beef stock

1 can (15 ounces) dark red kidney beans

1 can (28 ounces) diced tomatoes

1 can (10 ounces) tomatoes with green chiles and lime

2 tablespoons tomato paste

1. Place all ingredients, except beans, tomatoes and tomato paste into the pressure cooker; secure lid.
2. Set pressure cooker to STEW and timer to 30 minutes.
3. When cooking is complete, add remaining ingredients to pressure cooker; secure lid.
4. Set pressure cooker to SOUP and timer to 10 minutes.
5. When cooking is complete, serve immediately.

Traditional Chili

Makes 6 to 8 servings

Ingredients:

1 pound ground beef
1 pound ground pork
1 medium onion, chopped
3 garlic cloves, minced
1 chili pepper, finely chopped and seeds removed
1 envelope chili seasoning
1 can (28 ounces) crushed tomatoes
1 cup beef stock
1 teaspoon kosher salt
½ teaspoon black pepper
½ teaspoon cinnamon
1 can (15 ounces) dark red kidney beans, drained
Corn chips
Cheddar cheese, shredded
Green onions, chopped
Sour cream

1. Set pressure cooker to MEAT.
2. Add beef and pork to pressure cooker; cook for 5 minutes with the lid off, breaking apart the beef and pork with a wooden spoon.
3. Drain fat and place beef and pork back into pressure cooker.
4. Add remaining ingredients, except corn chips, cheese, green onions and sour cream to pressure cooker; secure lid.
5. Set pressure cooker to SOUP and timer to 20 minutes.
6. When cooking is complete, garnish with corn chips, cheese, green onions and sour cream.
7. Serve immediately.

Cabbage Soup

Ingredients:

2 medium onions, sliced

1 bell pepper, chopped

1 head of cabbage, sliced

2 broccoli stalks, chopped

½ cup mushrooms, sliced

1 turnip, peeled and diced

4 celery stalks, cut into 1-inch pieces

1 sprig rosemary

1 sprig thyme

2 garlic cloves, minced

4 cups beef stock

1 can (28 ounces) diced tomatoes

1 teaspoon salt

½ teaspoon freshly ground pepper

1 tablespoon balsamic vinegar

1. Place all ingredients into pressure cooker; secure lid.
2. Set pressure cooker to SOUP and timer to 30 minutes.
3. When cooking is complete, remove thyme and rosemary.
4. Serve immediately.

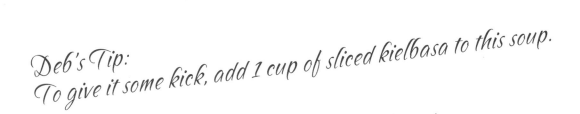

Deb's Tip:
To give it some kick, add 1 cup of sliced kielbasa to this soup.

Vegetable Stock

Ingredients:

4 medium onions, unpeeled and quartered

4 medium carrots, cut into 2-inch pieces

3 medium potatoes, halved

2 medium parsnips or turnips, cut into 2-inch pieces

1 small head of cabbage, cut into wedges

1 tablespoon extra-virgin olive oil

½ tablespoon salt

¼ teaspoon black pepper

8 cups water

1 sprig rosemary

1 tablespoon fresh oregano, chopped

1. Preheat oven to 350 degrees.
2. Place all vegetables on a roasting pan; drizzle with oil and sprinkle with salt and pepper.
3. Place pan in the oven and let roast for 30 minutes.
4. When roasting is complete, transfer pan contents and remaining ingredients to pressure cooker; secure lid.
5. Set pressure cooker to SOUP and timer to 20 minutes.
6. When cooking is complete, strain stock using a colander.
7. Refrigerate stock for up to 5 days.

Beef Stock

Ingredients:

2 pounds beef ribs

1 large onion, quartered

2 roma tomatoes, halved

1 turnip, halved

1 tablespoon extra-virgin olive oil

2 teaspoons kosher salt, divided

1 sprig thyme

1 sprig rosemary

1 bay leaf

4 cups water

1 cup dry red wine

1 teaspoon mixed peppercorns

1. Preheat oven to 400 degrees.
2. Place ribs on a roasting pan.
3. Add onions, tomatoes and turnips to pan; drizzle with oil and sprinkle with 1 teaspoon of salt.
4. Place pan in the oven and let roast for 40 minutes.
5. When roasting is complete, transfer pan contents to pressure cooker.
6. Add remaining ingredients to pressure cooker; secure lid.
7. Set pressure cooker to MEAT and timer to 45 minutes.
8. When cooking is complete, strain stock using a colander.
9. Refrigerate stock for 5 hours; remove hardened fat.

Deb's Tip:
Store stock in an airtight container and refrigerate for up to 1 week.

Fish Stock

Ingredients:

2 pounds snapper or grouper fish heads

1 medium onion, quartered

1 celery stalk

1 small carrot

2 sprigs thyme

6 whole peppercorns

½ tablespoon kosher salt

4 cups water

1. Place all ingredients into pressure cooker; secure lid.
2. Set pressure cooker to MEAT and timer to 15 minutes.
3. When cooking is complete, strain stock using a colander.
4. Cover and refrigerate.

Deb's Tip:
This stock can be stored in an airtight container for up to 1 week.

Rich Chicken Stock

Ingredients:

3 pounds chicken legs

1 medium onion, quartered

1 large carrot

1 celery stalk

1 turnip, quartered

1 sprig thyme

1 sprig rosemary

1 tablespoon extra-virgin olive oil

3 teaspoons kosher salt, divided

1 teaspoon freshly ground pepper

5 cups water

5 whole peppercorns

1. Preheat oven to 400 degrees.
2. Place chicken, vegetables and herbs on a roasting pan; drizzle with oil and sprinkle with 2 tablespoons salt and 1 teaspoon pepper.
3. Place pan in the oven and let roast for 40 minutes.
4. When roasting is complete, transfer pan contents to pressure cooker.
5. Add water, remaining salt and peppercorns to pressure cooker; secure lid.
6. Set pressure cooker to MEAT and timer to 45 minutes.
7. When cooking is complete, strain stock using a colander.
8. Refrigerate stock for 5 hours; remove hardened fat.

Vegetables

Function

Time   Delay Time

Keep Warm   Cancel

Spicy Green Beans

Ingredients:

1 pound green beans, trimmed and cut into 1-inch pieces

1 teaspoon salt

½ teaspoon freshly ground pepper

1 small onion, diced

1 small red bell pepper, diced

1 garlic clove, minced

2 medium tomatoes, diced

1 teaspoon lemon juice

½ cup chicken stock

2 tablespoons fresh cilantro, chopped

1. Place all ingredients, except cilantro, into pressure cooker; secure lid.
2. Set pressure cooker to VEGGIE and timer to 5 minutes.
3. When cooking is complete, sprinkle green beans with cilantro and serve.

Delicious Swiss Chard

Makes 2 to 4 servings

Ingredients:

2 bundles Swiss chard

½ cup water

1 teaspoon salt

1 teaspoon cider vinegar

1. Cut Swiss chard and stems into 2-inch pieces.
2. Place all ingredients into pressure cooker; secure lid.
3. Set pressure cooker to VEGGIE and timer to 5 minutes.
4. When cooking is complete, serve immediately.

Buttery Corn On The Cob

Ingredients:

6 ears of corn, husked

½ cup water

1 teaspoon salt

½ teaspoon sugar

3 tablespoons butter

1. Place all ingredients into pressure cooker; secure lid.
2. Set pressure cooker to VEGGIE and timer to 6 minutes.
3. When cooking is complete, stir and serve.

Deb's Tip:
Add some more salt and butter if desired.

Sesame Green Beans

Ingredients:

1 pound green beans, trimmed

½ cup chicken stock

½ teaspoon salt

½ teaspoon freshly ground pepper

2 teaspoons rice vinegar

1 teaspoon sesame oil

1 teaspoon sesame seeds

1. Place beans, stock, salt and pepper into pressure cooker; secure lid.
2. Set pressure cooker to SOUP and timer to 3 minutes.
3. In a bowl, combine remaining ingredients; stir well.
4. When cooking is complete, toss beans in vinegar mixture and serve.

Spaghetti Squash

Ingredients:

1 large spaghetti squash, seeds removed and cut horizontally

2 tablespoons butter, divided

¼ teaspoon kosher salt

¼ teaspoon black pepper

2 cups water

1. Place 1 tablespoon of butter on each squash half.
2. Sprinkle squash with salt and pepper.
3. Pour water into pressure cooker.
4. Fit pressure cooker with stainless rack and place squash on rack; secure lid.
5. Set pressure cooker to VEGGIE and timer to 30 minutes.
6. When cooking is complete, serve immediately.

Creamed Corn With Cilantro

Makes 4 to 6 servings

Ingredients:

8 ears of corn

1 cup chicken stock

1 teaspoon salt

½ teaspoon freshly ground pepper

1 teaspoon sugar

1 small onion, diced

1 tablespoon butter

1 tablespoon fresh cilantro, chopped

2 ounces cream cheese

1. Using a knife, remove corn from cobs.
2. Place corn kernels, cobs, stock, salt, pepper, sugar and onions into pressure cooker; secure lid.
3. Set pressure cooker to VEGGIE and timer to 10 minutes.
4. When cooking is complete, remove cobs.
5. Add butter, cilantro and cream cheese to pressure cooker; secure lid.
6. Set pressure cooker to VEGGIE and timer to 3 minutes.
7. When cooking is complete, puree corn using a blender until desired consistency.
8. Serve immediately.

Sweet Potato Casserole

Makes 4 to 6 servings

Ingredients:

4 sweet potatoes, peeled and quartered

1 cup chicken stock

½ cup orange juice

1 teaspoon salt

½ teaspoon freshly ground pepper

½ teaspoon cinnamon

2 tablespoons butter

Marshmallows

Non-stick cooking spray

1. Place all ingredients, except butter, marshmallows and non-stick spray, into pressure cooker; secure lid.
2. Set pressure cooker to VEGGIE and timer to 10 minutes.
3. When cooking is complete, drain potatoes, add butter and mash potatoes using a potato masher.
4. Set oven to broil.
5. Apply non-stick spray to an oven safe casserole and place mashed potatoes into casserole; top with marshmallows.
6. Place casserole on center rack in the oven and cook for 2 minutes or until marshmallows are lightly toasted.
7. Remove potatoes from oven and serve.

Nevar's Favorite Collard Greens

Ingredients:

1 smoked ham bone

4 cups water

1 medium onion, quartered

1 large bundle collard greens, washed and stems removed

1 teaspoon salt

½ teaspoon freshly ground pepper

½ teaspoon garlic powder

1 teaspoon pepper vinegar

1. Place ham bone, water and onions into pressure cooker; secure lid.
2. Set pressure cooker to MEAT and timer to 30 minutes.
3. When cooking is complete, cut ham off bone and place ham back into the pressure cooker; discard bone.
4. Add remaining ingredients to pressure cooker; secure lid.
5. Set pressure cooker to VEGGIE and timer to 15 minutes.
6. When cooking is complete, serve immediately.

Mashed Potatoes With Rutabaga

Ingredients:

6 yukon gold potatoes, peeled and halved

½ cup rutabaga, peeled and diced into 1-inch cubes

1 cup chicken stock

1 teaspoon salt

½ teaspoon freshly ground pepper

2 tablespoons heavy cream

2 tablespoons butter

1. Place all ingredients, except cream and butter, into pressure cooker; secure lid.
2. Set pressure cooker to VEGGIE and timer to 10 minutes.
3. When cooking is complete, drain potatoes.
4. Add cream and butter to potatoes and mash using a potato masher.
5. Serve immediately.

Mashed Potatoes

Ingredients:

1½ pounds yukon gold potatoes, peeled and halved

½ cup chicken stock

¼ cup heavy cream

3 tablespoons butter

1 teaspoon salt

½ teaspoon freshly ground pepper

⅛ teaspoon cinnamon

1. Place all ingredients into pressure cooker; secure lid.
2. Set pressure cooker to VEGGIE and timer to 10 minutes.
3. When cooking is complete, mash potatoes using a potato masher.
4. Serve immediately.

Corn Pudding

Ingredients:

2 cups water

Non-stick cooking spray

2-quart stainless steel bowl or baking insert

3 tablespoons butter, melted

4 ounces cream cheese, softened

1 box (8½ ounces) corn muffin mix

1 can (14¾ ounces) cream style corn

¾ cup sour cream

2 cups frozen corn

1 teaspoon salt

½ teaspoon freshly ground pepper

1. Pour water into pressure cooker.
2. Apply non-stick spray to stainless bowl.
3. Place remaining ingredients into stainless bowl; mix well.
4. Place stainless bowl into pressure cooker; secure lid.
5. Set pressure cooker to SOUP and timer to 15 minutes.
6. When cooking is complete, serve immediately.

Crazy Cola Carrots

Ingredients:

2½ pounds carrots, peeled and cut diagonally into 1-inch pieces

½ cup cola

1 teaspoon salt

½ teaspoon freshly ground pepper

1 tablespoon brown sugar

1 tablespoon butter

1. Place all ingredients into pressure cooker; secure lid.
2. Set pressure cooker to VEGGIE and timer to 7 minutes.
3. When cooking is complete, serve immediately.

Baked Beets In Butter

Makes 4 servings

Ingredients:

4 medium beets, washed, peeled and halved

Aluminum foil

2 teaspoons unsalted butter, divided

1 teaspoon salt

½ teaspoon freshly ground pepper

2 cups water

1. Top each beet with ½ teaspoon butter, salt and pepper.
2. Wrap each beet in aluminum foil.
3. Pour water into pressure cooker.
4. Fit pressure cooker with the stainless rack and place beets on rack; secure lid.
5. Set pressure cooker to VEGGIE and timer to 25 minutes.
6. When cooking is complete, serve immediately.

Braised Purple Cabbage

Ingredients:

1 head of purple cabbage, sliced

3 apples, cored and quartered

1 large onion, sliced

2 cups beef stock

1 teaspoon sugar

1 teaspoon salt

½ teaspoon freshly ground pepper

1 tablespoon balsamic vinegar

1 teaspoon caraway seeds

1. Place all ingredients, except caraway seeds, into pressure cooker; secure lid.
2. Set pressure cooker to VEGGIE and timer to 20 minutes.
3. When cooking is complete, add caraway seeds and serve.

Black Eyed Peas

Makes 6 to 8 servings

Ingredients:

1 pound dry black eyed peas

5 cups chicken stock

4 ounces smoked pork shoulder

1 medium onion, diced

1 tablespoon red wine vinegar

3 garlic cloves, minced

1 teaspoon salt

½ teaspoon freshly ground pepper

¼ teaspoon crushed red pepper flakes

1. Place all ingredients into pressure cooker; secure lid.
2. Set pressure cooker to RICE and timer to 20 minutes.
3. When cooking is complete, serve immediately.

Stuffed Artichokes

Ingredients:

4 medium artichokes

1 teaspoon salt

2 tablespoons lemon juice

2 cups chicken stock

1 tablespoon lemon zest

Stuffing:

4 garlic cloves, minced

1/3 cup extra-virgin olive oil

2 tablespoons fresh mint leaves, chopped

2 tablespoons fresh Italian parsley, chopped

2 tablespoons lemon juice

2 cups Italian breadcrumbs

1 cup Parmesan cheese, grated

1. Remove stems and outer leaves from artichokes; cut off 1-inch tops with scissors.
2. In a bowl, soak artichokes in water combined with salt and lemon juice.
3. In a separate bowl, combine stuffing ingredients; mix well.
4. Remove artichokes from bowl.
5. Using your fingers, spread leaves apart and fill with stuffing.
6. Fit pressure cooker with the stainless rack and place artichokes on rack.
7. Pour chicken stock over artichokes and sprinkle with zest; secure lid.
8. Set pressure cooker to VEGGIE and timer to 20 minutes.
9. When cooking is complete, serve immediately.

Tuscan Poached Onions

Ingredients:

4 medium sweet onions, peeled

2 cups chicken stock

2 teaspoons balsamic vinegar

1 teaspoon salt

½ teaspoon freshly ground pepper

2 sprigs thyme

1. Cut off the top and bottom of each onion.
2. Place onions and remaining ingredients into pressure cooker; secure lid.
3. Set pressure cooker to VEGGIE and timer to 10 minutes.
4. When cooking is complete, serve immediately.

Deb's Tip:
This makes the perfect side dish.

wolfgang puck
Bistro
collection

Rice
Beans &
Pastas

Function

Time   Delay Time

Keep Warm   Cancel

Red Beans With Rice

Makes 4 to 6 servings

Ingredients:

4 cups rice, cooked

1 pound dry red kidney beans, rinsed

1 large onion, diced

1 large bell pepper, diced

4 garlic cloves, chopped

1 large smoked ham hock

1½ pounds mild smoked sausage, sliced

2 teaspoons thyme

2 bay leaves

2 tablespoons parsley, chopped

½ teaspoon salt

½ teaspoon freshly ground pepper

½ teaspoon cayenne pepper

1 tablespoon hot sauce

1 teaspoon Worcestershire sauce

8 cups chicken stock

1. Place all ingredients, except rice, into pressure cooker; secure lid.
2. Set pressure cooker to MEAT and timer to 30 minutes.
3. When cooking is complete, remove bay leaves and serve over rice.

Deb's Tip:
To spice it up, use hot smoked sausage instead of the mild sausage.

Wild Rice with Mushrooms & Almonds

Ingredients:

2 cups wild rice, uncooked

4 cups beef stock

1 cup mushrooms, sliced

1 small onion, diced

2 tablespoons butter

½ cup almonds, slivered

2 tablespoons green onions, chopped

1. Place rice, stock, mushrooms and onions into pressure cooker; secure lid.
2. Set pressure cooker to RICE and timer to 30 minutes.
3. When cooking is complete, add butter and almonds; stir.
4. Garnish with green onions and serve.

Perfect Brown Rice

Ingredients:

1 pound long-grain brown rice, uncooked

5 cups water

1 teaspoon salt

1 tablespoon extra-virgin olive oil

1. Rinse rice and place into pressure cooker.
2. Add remaining ingredients to pressure cooker; secure lid.
3. Set pressure cooker to RICE and timer to 20 minutes.
4. When cooking is complete, serve immediately.

Cheesy Risotto With Broccoli

Makes 4 servings

Ingredients:

2 tablespoons extra-virgin olive oil

1 small onion, chopped

1 cup Arborio rice

1 teaspoon salt

1 cup chicken stock

1 cup milk

1 cup Cheddar cheese, shredded

¾ cup broccoli flowerets

1. Place all ingredients, except cheese and broccoli, into pressure cooker; secure lid.
2. Set pressure cooker to RICE and timer to 6 minutes.
3. When cooking is complete, add cheese to pressure cooker; stir well.
4. Add broccoli to pressure cooker; secure lid.
5. Set pressure cooker to VEGGIE and timer to 3 minutes.
6. When cooking is complete, serve immediately.

Brown Rice Pilaf With Lentils

Makes 4 to 6 servings

Ingredients:

1 cup brown basmati rice, uncooked

1 cup water

1 teaspoon salt

1 tablespoon extra-virgin olive oil

1 cup lentils

2 garlic cloves, minced

2 carrots, peeled and diced

1 medium onion, diced

1 cup tomatoes, diced

2 cups vegetable stock

1 tablespoon fresh parsley, chopped

1. Place rice, water, salt and oil into pressure cooker; secure lid.
2. Set pressure cooker to RICE and timer to 15 minutes.
3. When cooking is complete, add remaining ingredients, except parsley, to pressure cooker; secure lid.
4. Set pressure cooker to RICE and timer to 6 minutes.
5. When cooking is complete, stir well.
6. Top with parsley and serve.

Black Beans

Ingredients:

1 pound dry black beans

5 cups beef stock

1 medium onion, diced

2 garlic cloves, minced

1 red bell pepper, diced

2 tablespoons fresh cilantro, chopped

1 teaspoon salt

½ teaspoon freshly ground pepper

1 teaspoon cumin

1 can (14½ ounces) petite diced tomatoes with olive oil

1. Place all ingredients into pressure cooker; secure lid.
2. Set pressure cooker to MEAT and timer to 50 minutes.
3. When cooking is complete, serve immediately.

Deb's Tip:
Serve beans with a touch of red wine vinegar over rice and top it off with freshly chopped green onions.

Hummus

Ingredients:

1 cup dried garbanzo beans

1 teaspoon baking soda

1 lemon, juice and zest

2 garlic cloves, minced

1 teaspoon cumin

3 teaspoons salt

½ teaspoon cayenne pepper

5 cups water

2 tablespoons Tahini paste

1 cup extra-virgin olive oil

1. In a bowl, cover garbanzo beans with water and baking soda; let soak for 1 hour.
2. Rinse beans and transfer to pressure cooker.
3. Add lemon juice, zest, garlic, cumin, salt, cayenne pepper and 5 cups of water to pressure cooker; secure lid.
4. Set pressure cooker to MEAT and timer to 30 minutes.
5. When cooking is complete, drain beans.
6. Transfer beans to a food processor fitted with a metal chopping blade and add Tahini paste.
7. Process beans and slowly add the oil to create an emulsion.
8. Transfer hummus to a plate and serve.

Deb's Tip:
Great with warm pita bread.

Macaroni & Cheese

Makes 4 to 6 servings

Ingredients:

2½ cups dry elbow macaroni

2 cups chicken stock

1 cup heavy cream

1 teaspoon salt

1 teaspoon freshly ground pepper

1 tablespoon butter

½ cup milk

1½ cups Cheddar cheese, shredded

1½ cups Mozzarella cheese, shredded

1. Place macaroni, stock, cream, salt and pepper into pressure cooker; secure lid.
2. Set pressure cooker to RICE and timer to 8 minutes.
3. When cooking is complete, add remaining ingredients to pressure cooker and stir until creamy.
4. Serve immediately.

Pasta With Hot Italian Sausage

Makes 4 to 6 servings

Ingredients:

1½ pounds hot Italian sausage in casings

½ cup water

1 box (1 pound) dry rigatoni pasta

3 cups chicken stock

3 cups pasta sauce

2 cups Ricotta cheese

2 cups Mozzarella cheese, shredded

1 teaspoon garlic powder

1 teaspoon salt

1 teaspoon black pepper

1. Place sausage and water into pressure cooker; secure lid.
2. Set pressure cooker to RICE and timer to 10 minutes.
3. When cooking is complete, remove sausage and drain excess liquid.
4. Slice the sausage and place it back into the pressure cooker.
5. Add remaining ingredients to pressure cooker; secure lid.
6. Set pressure cooker to RICE and timer to 20 minutes.
7. When cooking is complete, serve immediately.

Deb's Tip:
Serve this pasta with warm garlic bread.

Deb's Famous Meaty Pasta

Ingredients:

1 pound frozen ground beef

3 cups dry penne or ziti pasta

2½ cups beef stock

3 cups pasta sauce

1 teaspoon salt

½ teaspoon freshly ground pepper

1 teaspoon Italian seasoning

½ teaspoon garlic powder

½ cup Mozzarella cheese, shredded

1. Place all ingredients into pressure cooker; secure lid.
2. Set pressure cooker to MEAT and timer to 20 minutes.
3. When cooking is complete, break meat apart using a rubber spatula, stir and serve.

wolfgang puck
Bistro
collection

Beef
Lamb &
Pork

Function

Time   Delay Time

Keep Warm   Cancel

Beef Stroganoff

Ingredients:

2 cups noodles, cooked and buttered

1 tablespoon flour

1 teaspoon salt

½ teaspoon freshly ground pepper

1 pound beef sirloin, cut into 1-inch pieces

1 medium onion, chopped

2 garlic cloves, minced

1 pound mushrooms, sliced

1 sprig thyme

1 cup beef stock

1 teaspoon Worcestershire sauce

1 cup sour cream

1. In a bowl, combine flour, salt and pepper.
2. Roll beef pieces in flour mixture; shake off excess.
3. Add beef and remaining ingredients, except sour cream and noodles, to pressure cooker; secure lid.
4. Set pressure cooker to STEW and timer to 20 minutes.
5. When cooking is complete, remove thyme and stir in sour cream.
6. Serve over buttered noodles.

Porcupine Balls

Ingredients:

1 pound ground chuck

½ cup white rice, uncooked

½ cup water

1 small onion, minced

1 teaspoon salt

½ teaspoon celery salt

¼ teaspoon garlic powder

½ teaspoon freshly ground pepper

1½ cups beef stock

2 cups tomato sauce

2 teaspoons Worcestershire sauce

1. In a bowl, combine chuck, rice, water, onions and seasonings.
2. Shape meat mixture into 2-inch balls.
3. Add meatballs and beef stock to pressure cooker; secure lid.
4. Set pressure cooker to RICE and timer to 15 minutes.
5. When cooking is complete, transfer porcupine balls to a platter.
6. Add tomato sauce and Worcestershire sauce to pressure cooker.
7. With the lid open, set pressure cooker to RICE and let sauce heat through.
8. Place porcupine balls back into pressure cooker, stir and serve.

BBQ Beef Brisket

Ingredients:

3 pound beef brisket, trimmed

1 cup beef stock

1 cup apple cider

1 teaspoon cider vinegar

1 teaspoon salt

½ teaspoon freshly ground pepper

2 cups barbecue sauce

1. Place all ingredients, except barbecue sauce, into pressure cooker; secure lid.
2. Set pressure cooker to MEAT and timer to 1 hour.
3. When cooking is complete, remove brisket and press MEAT again; let liquid reduce for 10 minutes with the lid off.
4. Cut brisket into pieces and place meat back into pressure cooker.
5. Add barbecue sauce to pressure cooker; let heat and serve.

Deb's Tip:
This makes a delicious sandwich on Texas toast.

Braised Beef Ribs

Ingredients:

2 pounds beef short ribs

1 medium onion, diced

2 garlic cloves, minced

2 tablespoons cherry jam

1 tablespoon tomato paste

1 cup beef stock

1 teaspoon Italian seasoning

1 teaspoon salt

½ teaspoon freshly ground pepper

1. Place all ingredients into pressure cooker; secure lid.
2. Set pressure cooker to MEAT and timer to 40 minutes.
3. When cooking is complete, remove lid.
4. Press MEAT again and cook for 10 minutes or until sauce is thickened.
5. Serve immediately.

Corned Beef & Cabbage

Makes 4 to 6 servings

Ingredients:

3 pound corned beef, trimmed

1 large onion, quartered

½ cup beef stock

1 bottle (12 ounces) beer

½ teaspoon mustard seeds

½ teaspoon whole peppercorns

2 allspice berries

1 bay leaf

1 teaspoon mustard powder

3 garlic cloves, minced

6 small onions, peeled

6 small bliss potatoes, halved

12 baby carrots

1 head of cabbage, cut into 6 wedges

1. Place all ingredients, except small onions, potatoes, carrots and cabbage, into pressure cooker; secure lid.
2. Set pressure cooker to MEAT and timer to 70 minutes.
3. When cooking is complete, remove bay leaf.
4. Add remaining ingredients to pressure cooker; secure lid.
5. Set pressure cooker to VEGGIE and timer to 7 minutes.
6. When cooking is complete, serve immediately.

Deb's Tip:
Serve this with creamy horseradish sauce on the side.

Beef Enchiladas

Ingredients:

1 flank steak
1 cup beef stock
1 enchilada dinner kit
1 cup Cheddar cheese, shredded
Sour cream
Green onions, chopped

1. Place steak, stock and seasoning mix from the dinner kit into pressure cooker; secure lid.
2. Set pressure cooker to MEAT and timer to 1 hour.
3. When cooking is complete, shred steak using 2 forks.
4. Lay the tortillas from the dinner kit on a cutting board and sprinkle with cheese.
5. Add shredded steak to each tortilla and roll up.
6. Pour enchilada sauce from the dinner kit over enchiladas and top with cheese.
7. Microwave enchiladas for 1 minute or until cheese is melted.
8. Garnish with sour cream and green onions.
9. Serve immediately.

Braciole

Ingredients:

1 pound top sirloin, sliced very thin

½ cup butter, melted

1½ cups Parmesan cheese, grated

1½ cups soft breadcrumbs

1 teaspoon salt

½ teaspoon freshly ground pepper

1 tablespoon fresh parsley, chopped

½ teaspoon garlic salt

½ cup raisins

Toothpicks

½ cup red wine

1 cup beef stock

1 sprig thyme

3 cups pasta sauce

1. Lay steak slices flat on a cutting board.
2. In a bowl, combine butter, cheese, breadcrumbs, salt, pepper, parsley, garlic salt and raisins; mix well.
3. Place 2 tablespoons raisin mixture on the bottom corner of each steak slice; roll up and secure with a toothpick.
4. Add meat rolls, wine, stock and thyme to pressure cooker; secure lid.
5. Set pressure cooker to MEAT and timer to 20 minutes.
6. When cooking is complete, remove thyme, add pasta sauce and let sauce heat through.
7. Serve immediately.

Ropa Vieja

Ingredients:

2 pounds flank steak

1 medium onion, peeled and halved

4 garlic cloves, minced

1 cup beef stock

1 teaspoon cumin

½ teaspoon coriander

1 envelope Latin seasoning

½ cup red wine

1 can (14½ ounces) petite diced tomatoes

1 green bell pepper, diced

2 tablespoons cilantro, chopped

¼ cup capers, drained

1. Place steak, onions, garlic, stock, cumin, coriander, Latin seasoning and wine into pressure cooker; secure lid.
2. Set pressure cooker to MEAT and timer to 40 minutes.
3. When cooking is complete, shred meat using 2 forks and add remaining ingredients to pressure cooker; secure lid.
4. Set pressure cooker to MEAT and timer to 20 minutes.
5. When cooking is complete, serve immediately.

Italian Style Meatloaf

Ingredients:

1 medium onion, minced

3 garlic cloves, minced

¼ cup fresh breadcrumbs

¼ cup heavy cream

2 large eggs, beaten

1½ pounds ground chuck

½ pound ground pork

¼ cup Parmesan cheese, grated

1 tablespoon Italian seasoning

1 teaspoon salt

1 teaspoon freshly ground pepper

2 cups beef stock

2 cups pasta sauce, divided

1 cup Mozzarella cheese, shredded

1. In a bowl, combine onions, garlic, breadcrumbs, cream and eggs; mix well and let rest for 5 minutes.
2. Add chuck, pork, Parmesan cheese, Italian seasoning, salt and pepper to bowl; mix well and shape mixture into a loaf.
3. Pour beef stock into pressure cooker.
4. Fit pressure cooker with stainless rack and place loaf on rack; cover loaf with 1 cup of pasta sauce and secure lid.
5. Set pressure cooker to MEAT and timer to 20 minutes.
6. When cooking is complete, pour remaining pasta sauce over loaf and top with Mozzarella cheese; secure lid.
7. Set pressure cooker to VEGGIE and timer to 10 minutes.
8. When cooking is complete, serve immediately.

Stuffed Flank Steak

Makes 4 servings

Ingredients:

2 pounds flank steak

1 bell pepper, cut into strips

1 small onion, cut into strips

3 slices Mozzarella cheese

Butcher's twine

1 tablespoon extra-virgin olive oil

1 teaspoon Italian seasoning

1 teaspoon salt

½ teaspoon black pepper

2 cups beef stock

1 can (14½ ounces) Italian seasoned stewed tomatoes

1. Open steak and place peppers, onions and cheese on steak.
2. Roll up steak and tie with twine.
3. Rub rolls with oil, Italian seasoning, salt and pepper.
4. Add rolls, stock and stewed tomatoes to pressure cooker; secure lid.
5. Set pressure cooker to MEAT and timer to 45 minutes.
6. When cooking is complete, remove rolls, discard twine and cut steak into ½-inch slices.
7. Place steak slices on a platter, pour sauce from pressure cooker over steak and serve.

Deb's Tip:
Serve with rice or pasta.

Beef Goulash

Ingredients:

2 pounds stew beef

1 medium onion, sliced

2 garlic cloves, minced

1½ cups beef stock

½ cup ketchup

2 tablespoons Worcestershire sauce

1 tablespoon brown sugar

2 teaspoons salt

2 teaspoons paprika

1 tablespoon caraway seeds

1. Place all ingredients into pressure cooker; secure lid.
2. Set pressure cooker to STEW and timer to 35 minutes.
3. When cooking is complete, serve immediately.

Deb's Tip:
Serve over spatzle.

Beef Pot Roast

Makes 4 to 6 servings

Ingredients:

1 teaspoon salt

½ teaspoon freshly ground pepper

3 pound chuck roast

2 cups beef stock

1 cup tomato juice

2 small onions, peeled and halved

1 sprig thyme

1 sprig rosemary

1 tablespoon Worcestershire sauce

8 new potatoes, halved

4 carrots, peeled and cut into 2-inch pieces

1. Place all ingredients, except potatoes and carrots, into pressure cooker; secure lid.
2. Set pressure cooker to MEAT and timer to 1 hour.
3. When cooking is complete, remove thyme and rosemary.
4. Add potatoes and carrots to pressure cooker; secure lid.
5. Set pressure cooker to VEGGIE and timer to 5 minutes.
6. When cooking is complete, serve immediately.

Steaks In A Snap

Ingredients:

2 frozen sirloin steaks

1½ cups red wine

1 medium onion, sliced

8 ounces mushrooms, sliced

1 envelope French onion soup mix

2 medium russet potatoes, wrapped in foil

1. Place all ingredients, except potatoes, into pressure cooker.
2. Fit pressure cooker with stainless rack and place potatoes on rack; secure lid.
3. Set pressure cooker to MEAT and timer to 25 minutes.
4. When cooking is complete, serve immediately.

Braised Lamb Shanks

Ingredients:

4 meaty lamb shanks, cut into 3-inch pieces

1 teaspoon kosher salt

½ teaspoon black pepper

1 teaspoon fresh rosemary, chopped

3 tablespoons extra-virgin olive oil

1 medium onion, chopped

2 medium carrots, peeled and chopped

2 garlic cloves, minced

½ cup dry red wine

1 cup diced tomatoes, drained

2 cups beef stock

1. Season lamb shanks with salt, pepper and rosemary.
2. Place lamb shanks and remaining ingredients into pressure cooker; secure lid.
3. Set pressure cooker to MEAT and timer to 45 minutes.
4. When cooking is complete, serve immediately.

Osso Buco

Ingredients:

2 pounds meaty veal shanks

½ cup onions, diced

½ cup celery, diced

½ cup parsnips, diced

2 garlic cloves, minced

1 teaspoon salt

½ teaspoon freshly ground pepper

½ cup vermouth

1 can (14½ ounces) petite diced tomatoes

1 sprig thyme

1 teaspoon orange zest

1 cup beef stock

1. Place all ingredients into pressure cooker; secure lid.
2. Set pressure cooker to MEAT and timer to 40 minutes.
3. When cooking is complete, remove thyme and transfer veal to a platter.
4. With the lid off, set pressure cooker to MEAT and reduce the sauce for 10 minutes.
5. Using a blender, puree the sauce, pour it over veal shanks and serve.

Meatballs For Spaghetti

Makes 6 to 8 servings

Meatballs:

1½ cups fresh breadcrumbs

4 cups beef stock, divided

1 pound ground chuck

½ pound ground pork

3 garlic cloves, minced

1 small onion, minced

¾ cup Romano cheese, grated

1 teaspoon salt

½ teaspoon freshly ground pepper

2 large eggs, beaten

Sauce:

4 tablespoons extra-virgin olive oil

4 tablespoons tomato paste

2 cans (28 ounces each) Italian tomatoes

3 garlic cloves, minced

1 small onion, minced

1 teaspoon dry oregano

1 teaspoon dried basil

1. In a bowl, soak breadcrumbs in 2 cups of beef stock.
2. Pour remaining stock into pressure cooker and set to MEAT.
3. Add remaining meatball ingredients to breadcrumbs; mix and form mixture into 2-inch meatballs.
4. Place meatballs into pressure cooker; secure lid.
5. Set pressure cooker to MEAT and timer to 20 minutes.
6. When cooking is complete, transfer meatballs to a platter and pour stock into a separate bowl; skim off the fat.
7. Dissolve tomato paste in the strained stock and pour it into the pressure cooker.
8. Add remaining sauce ingredients and meatballs to pressure cooker; secure lid.
9. Set pressure cooker to STEW and timer to 15 minutes.
10. When cooking is complete, serve over spaghetti.

Baby Back Ribs

Ingredients:

3 tablespoons rice wine vinegar

1 tablespoon soy sauce

½ cup orange juice

1 teaspoon garlic salt

3 garlic cloves, minced

1 tablespoon brown sugar

1 teaspoon salt

½ teaspoon freshly ground pepper

1 slab baby back ribs, cut into pieces

1 cup ginger ale soda

2 cups barbecue sauce

1. In a bowl, combine vinegar, soy sauce, orange juice, garlic salt, garlic, sugar, salt and pepper.
2. Place ribs into the bowl and let marinate for 1 hour.
3. Add ribs, marinade and ginger ale to pressure cooker; secure lid.
4. Set pressure cooker to MEAT and timer to 20 minutes.
5. When cooking is complete, add barbecue sauce to pressure cooker; stir well.
6. Serve immediately.

Deb's Tip:
For a crunchier texture, place ribs under the broiler before adding the BBQ sauce.

BBQ Pulled Pork

Makes 6 to 8 servings

Ingredients:

4 pound boneless pork butt roast

1 teaspoon kosher salt

1 teaspoon garlic salt

1 teaspoon sweet paprika

1 teaspoon black pepper

2 teaspoons soy sauce

2 cups apple cider

1 bottle (16 ounces) barbecue sauce

1 tablespoon cider vinegar

Sandwich rolls

1. Place all ingredients, except barbecue sauce, vinegar, and sandwich rolls, into pressure cooker; secure lid.
2. Set pressure cooker to MEAT and timer to 1 hour.
3. When cooking is complete, remove roast, cut into slices and place them back into the pressure cooker.
4. Add barbecue sauce and vinegar to pressure cooker; secure lid.
5. Set pressure cooker to MEAT and timer to 20 minutes.
6. When cooking is complete, serve on sandwich rolls.

Deb's Tip:
To add some crunch, top your sandwich with coleslaw.

Pork Carnitas

Ingredients:

2 pound boneless pork center rib, cut into 2-inch cubes

½ cup orange juice

½ cup chicken stock

2 garlic cloves, chopped

1 small onion, diced

1 bay leaf

1 sprig thyme

1 teaspoon salt

½ teaspoon freshly ground pepper

Lettuce leaves

Salsa

1. Place all ingredients, except lettuce leaves and salsa, into pressure cooker; secure lid.
2. Set pressure cooker to MEAT and timer to 40 minutes.
3. When cooking is complete, remove bay leaf and thyme.
4. Wrap meat in lettuce leaves like a taco, top with salsa and serve.

Pork With Apples

Ingredients:

2 pound boneless pork loin

1 teaspoon salt

½ teaspoon freshly ground pepper

½ teaspoon fennel seeds

1 shallot, chopped

2 large apples, cored and sliced

½ cup chicken stock

½ cup apple cider

1 cinnamon stick

1. Season pork with salt and pepper.
2. Place pork and remaining ingredients into pressure cooker; secure lid.
3. Set pressure cooker to MEAT and timer to 50 minutes.
4. When cooking is complete, remove cinnamon stick.
5. Serve pork and apples on a platter with a ladle of the cooking liquid.

Pork Chops Dijon

Ingredients:

4 bone-in pork chops, cut 2-inches thick

½ cup chicken stock

1 tablespoon dijon mustard

½ cup orange juice

1 teaspoon salt

1 teaspoon freshly ground pepper

1 can (10¾ ounces) golden mushroom soup

1. Place all ingredients into pressure cooker; secure lid.
2. Set pressure cooker to MEAT and timer to 20 minutes.
3. When cooking is complete, transfer pork chops to a platter.
4. Stir sauce until smooth, pour over pork chops and serve.

Pork Chili Verde

Ingredients:

2 pounds boneless pork, cut into 2-inch cubes

1 cup chicken stock

1 can (4 ounces) green chiles, chopped

4 whole tomatillos, husks removed and chopped

1 tablespoon fresh lime juice

1 teaspoon salt

½ teaspoon freshly ground pepper

1 teaspoon cumin

1 teaspoon coriander

2 garlic cloves, minced

1 small onion, chopped

3 tablespoons cilantro, chopped

Sour cream

1. Place all ingredients, except cilantro and sour cream, into pressure cooker; secure lid.
2. Set pressure cooker to STEW and timer to 40 minutes.
3. When cooking is complete, sprinkle with cilantro.
4. Serve in bowls topped with sour cream.

Deb's Tip:
This meat is perfect for enchiladas.

Sunday Gravy

Ingredients:

1 pound lean pork chops, bone-in

1 pound lean beef stew meat

1 pound Italian sausage, casings removed

1 piece (1-inch) pepperoni

¼ cup extra-virgin olive oil

3 garlic cloves, minced

1 cup beef stock

1 teaspoon salt

½ teaspoon freshly ground pepper

2 cans (28 ounces each) whole peeled tomatoes

3 tablespoons tomato paste

1. Place pork chops, stew meat, sausage, pepperoni, oil, garlic and stock into pressure cooker; secure lid.

2. Set pressure cooker to MEAT and timer to 40 minutes.

3. When cooking is complete, ladle out half of the beef stock and set aside.

4. Add salt, pepper and peeled tomatoes to pressure cooker.

5. In a bowl, dissolve tomato paste in the reserved beef stock and pour into pressure cooker; secure lid.

6. Set pressure cooker to STEW and timer to 15 minutes.

7. When cooking is complete, serve immediately.

Deb's Tip:
I love to serve this Italian meat sauce at parties with differently cooked pastas. All you need is salad and garlic bread to make a perfect Italian meal.

Ribs & Kraut

Ingredients:

1 tablespoon extra-virgin olive oil

3 pounds spare ribs, cut into individual ribs

1 teaspoon salt

½ teaspoon freshly ground pepper

½ cup chicken stock

½ teaspoon caraway seeds

3 carrots, peeled and cut into 2-inch pieces

4 small red bliss potatoes

1 small onion, quartered

1 jar (32 ounces) sauerkraut, drained

1. Place all ingredients into pressure cooker; secure lid.
2. Set pressure cooker to MEAT and timer to 20 minutes.
3. When cooking is complete, serve immediately.

Swedish Meatballs

Ingredients:

1½ cups breadcrumbs

½ cup heavy cream

1 pound ground chuck

½ pound ground pork

2 large eggs, beaten

1 small onion, minced

1 celery stalk, minced

2 teaspoons salt

½ teaspoon freshly ground pepper

¼ teaspoon ground allspice

2 cups beef stock

1 cup sour cream

1. In a large bowl, soak breadcrumbs in heavy cream for 5 minutes.
2. Add remaining ingredients, except stock and sour cream, to bowl; mix well.
3. Shape mixture into 1-inch meatballs.
4. Add meatballs and stock to pressure cooker; secure lid.
5. Set pressure cooker to MEAT and timer to 20 minutes.
6. When cooking is complete, transfer meatballs to a platter.
7. Add sour cream to sauce in pressure cooker, stir and pour over meatballs.
8. Serve immediately.

Deb's Tip:
This is best served over buttered noodles.

Stuffed Cabbage Rolls

Ingredients:

½ pound ground chuck

½ pound ground pork

1 small onion, chopped

½ cup white rice, uncooked

½ teaspoon thyme leaves

1 cup Swiss cheese, shredded

8 large cabbage leaves

Toothpicks

1 cup beef stock

1 can (15 ounces) tomato sauce

1 teaspoon sugar

1 teaspoon oregano

½ teaspoon garlic powder

1 tablespoon cider vinegar

1. In a bowl, combine meats, onions, rice, thyme and cheese; mix well.
2. Place ⅓ cup of meat mixture onto each leaf; fold in the sides and roll up.
3. Secure rolls with toothpicks and place them into the pressure cooker.
4. In a bowl, combine remaining ingredients and pour into pressure cooker; secure lid.
5. Set pressure cooker to MEAT and timer to 20 minutes.
6. When cooking is complete, serve immediately.

wolfgang puck
Bistro
collection

Chicken & Turkey

Function

Time   Delay Time

Keep Warm   Cancel

Chicken & Yellow Rice

Ingredients:

1 bag (16 ounces) yellow rice

4 boneless, skinless chicken breasts, cubed

2 tablespoons extra-virgin olive oil

1 teaspoon salt

½ teaspoon freshly ground pepper

4 cups water

1 cup frozen peas

½ cup Spanish olives

1. Place all ingredients, except olives, into pressure cooker; secure lid.
2. Set pressure cooker to RICE and timer to 20 minutes.
3. When cooking is complete, add olives and serve.

Chicken Enchilada Casserole

Makes 4 to 6 servings

Ingredients:

2 pounds boneless, skinless chicken breasts

1 can (4 ounces) green chiles, chopped

1 envelope taco seasoning

1 cup chicken stock

1 can (18.6 ounces) tortilla soup

12 tortilla chips

1 can (10 ounces) enchilada sauce

1 cup Colby and Cheddar cheese blend, shredded

3 green onions, chopped

Sour cream

1. Place chicken, chiles, taco seasoning, stock and tortilla soup into pressure cooker; secure lid.
2. Set pressure cooker to STEW and timer to 15 minutes.
3. When cooking is complete, add tortilla chips, enchilada sauce and cheese; stir and secure lid.
4. Set pressure cooker to VEGGIE and timer to 3 minutes.
5. When cooking is complete, garnish with green onions and sour cream.
6. Serve immediately.

Chicken & Dumplings

Makes 4 to 6 servings

Ingredients:

2 pounds boneless, skinless chicken

2 cups chicken stock

1 sprig thyme

1 teaspoon kosher salt

½ teaspoon freshly ground pepper

4 large carrots, peeled and sliced into 1-inch pieces

1 large onion, diced

3 celery stalks, sliced

1 can (10¾ ounces) cream of chicken soup

1 can (7½ ounces) Pop N' Fresh biscuit dough, cut into squares

2 tablespoons fresh parsley, chopped

1. Place chicken, stock, thyme, salt and pepper into pressure cooker; secure lid.
2. Set pressure cooker to MEAT and timer to 20 minutes.
3. When cooking is complete, remove thyme.
4. Add carrots, onions and celery to pressure cooker; secure lid.
5. Set pressure cooker to SOUP and timer to 5 minutes.
6. When cooking is complete, remove lid and set pressure cooker to SOUP; stir in cream of chicken soup.
7. When liquid starts to simmer, add biscuit squares and cover with the glass lid; steam for 5 minutes.
8. When cooking is complete, sprinkle with parsley and serve.

Chicken Pot Pie Towers

Ingredients:

1 box puff pastry shells

2 pounds skinless chicken breasts, bone-in

1 cup chicken stock

1 medium onion, halved

1 sprig thyme

1 teaspoon salt

½ teaspoon freshly ground pepper

1 can (10¾ ounces) cream of mushroom soup

1½ cups frozen mixed vegetables

1. Prepare shells according to package directions.
2. Place chicken, stock, onions, thyme, salt and pepper into pressure cooker; secure lid.
3. Set pressure cooker to MEAT and timer to 20 minutes.
4. When cooking is complete, remove thyme.
5. Remove chicken meat from bones and place chicken meat back into the pressure cooker.
6. Add soup and vegetables to pressure cooker; secure lid.
7. Set pressure cooker to MEAT and timer to 5 minutes.
8. When cooking is complete, place a scoop of chicken mixture in the center of each shell and serve.

Chicken Piccata

Ingredients:

4 boneless, skinless chicken breasts

½ teaspoon garlic salt

½ teaspoon freshly ground pepper

1 shallot, minced

1 lemon, juice and zest

1 cup white wine

1 tablespoon fresh parsley, chopped

1 tablespoon green olives, sliced

1 envelope chicken gravy

1. Place all ingredients into pressure cooker; secure lid.
2. Set pressure cooker to MEAT and timer to 10 minutes.
3. When cooking is complete, transfer chicken to a platter, pour sauce over chicken and serve.

Chicken Marsala

Ingredients:

4 frozen boneless, skinless chicken breasts

1 cup mushrooms, sliced

1 shallot, sliced

½ cup chicken stock

½ cup marsala wine

1 sprig thyme

1 teaspoon salt

½ teaspoon freshly ground pepper

1 envelope brown gravy mix

1. Place all ingredients into pressure cooker; secure lid.
2. Set pressure cooker to MEAT and timer to 20 minutes.
3. When cooking is complete, remove thyme.
4. Transfer chicken to a platter, pour sauce over chicken and serve.

Chicken Tacos

Ingredients:

3 frozen boneless, skinless chicken breasts

1 box taco dinner kit

1 cup chicken stock

1 teaspoon lime zest

1 cup lettuce, shredded

1 tomato, diced

3 green onions, chopped

½ cup Cheddar cheese, shredded

½ cup sour cream

1. Place chicken, taco seasoning from dinner kit, stock and lime zest into pressure cooker; secure lid.
2. Set pressure cooker to MEAT and timer to 20 minutes.
3. When cooking is complete, shred chicken using 2 forks.
4. Make a large platter with lettuce, tomatoes, green onions, cheese, sour cream, chicken, taco sauce and shells.
5. Let everyone dress their tacos the way they like.

Chicken Paprika

Ingredients:

4 boneless, skinless chicken breasts, cut into 2-inch pieces

1 large onion, chopped

1 teaspoon salt

½ teaspoon freshly ground pepper

1 tablespoon sweet paprika

1 cup chicken stock

1 can (14½ ounces) diced tomatoes with green peppers

1 cup heavy cream

1 tablespoon sour cream

1. Place all ingredients, except sour cream, into pressure cooker; secure lid.
2. Set pressure cooker to STEW and timer to 20 minutes.
3. When cooking is complete, stir in sour cream and serve.

Deb's Tip:
This dish is best served over wide egg noodles.

Coq Au Vin

Ingredients:

1 whole chicken, cut into pieces

1 tablespoon flour

1 teaspoon salt

½ teaspoon freshly ground pepper

2 bacon strips, diced

2 tablespoons butter

8 boiler onions, peeled

1 pound whole mushrooms

2 sprigs thyme

2 cups dry red wine

1 cup chicken stock

1 teaspoon sugar

1. Rub chicken with flour, salt and pepper.
2. In a skillet on medium heat, cook bacon until crisp.
3. Add butter to skillet; let melt.
4. Add chicken pieces to skillet; cook until golden brown.
5. Transfer skillet contents and remaining ingredients to pressure cooker; secure lid.
6. Set pressure cooker to STEW and timer to 40 minutes.
7. When cooking is complete, transfer chicken, onions and mushrooms to a platter.
8. With the lid off, set pressure cooker to STEW again and reduce liquid for 10 minutes.
9. Ladle sauce over chicken and serve.

Stuffed Turkey Breast

Makes 4 to 6 servings

Ingredients:

2 pounds turkey breast tenderloins, butterflied
½ teaspoon salt
¼ teaspoon poultry seasoning
1 box (6 ounces) turkey flavored stuffing mix
½ cup dried cherries
Toothpicks
1 cup chicken stock
1 envelope turkey gravy

1. Sprinkle turkey with salt and poultry seasoning.
2. Prepare stuffing mix according to package directions and add the dried cherries to the stuffing.
3. Divide the stuffing between the tenderloins and place mixture in the center of each tenderloin.
4. Roll tenderloins to cover the stuffing and secure with toothpicks.
5. Add stock and gravy envelope to pressure cooker.
6. Place turkey, toothpick side down, into pressure cooker; secure lid.
7. Set pressure cooker to MEAT and timer to 20 minutes.
8. When cooking is complete, transfer turkey to a cutting board.
9. Remove toothpicks, slice turkey into 1-inch rounds and serve with gravy.

Deb's Tip:
Try dried cranberries instead of the cherries.

Desserts

Function

Time   Delay Time

Keep Warm   Cancel

Mixed Berry Cobbler

Ingredients:

Non-stick cooking spray

2-quart stainless steel bowl or baking insert

1 bag (12 ounces) frozen mixed berries

¾ cup sugar

3 teaspoons quick cook tapioca

1 teaspoon orange zest

2 cups water

Aluminum foil

Topping:

2 cups Buttermilk Biscuit mix

⅓ cup milk

3 tablespoons sugar

3 tablespoons unsalted butter, melted

1 teaspoon vanilla

1. Apply non-stick spray to stainless bowl.
2. Place berries, sugar, tapioca and orange zest into bowl; mix well.
3. In a separate bowl, combine topping ingredients, mix well and pour over berry mixture; cover with foil.
4. Pour water into pressure cooker and add stainless bowl; secure lid.
5. Set pressure cooker to SOUP and timer to 25 minutes.
6. When cooking is complete, serve hot or cold.

Deb's Tip:
Serve over vanilla ice cream.

Creamy Cheesecake

Makes 4 to 6 servings

Ingredients:

Parchment paper

6-inch springform pan

Non-stick cooking spray

¾ cup sugar

2 packages (8 ounces each) cream cheese

1 tablespoon lemon juice

1 teaspoon vanilla

2 tablespoons flour

1 cup sour cream

2 large eggs

Aluminum foil

2 cups water

1. Place a piece of parchment paper on the base of the springform pan; assemble and secure the springform pan.

2. Apply non-stick spray to springform pan.

3. Using a mixer, cream the cream cheese and sugar until smooth.

4. Add lemon juice, vanilla, flour and sour cream to cream cheese mixture.

5. Add eggs, one at a time, and mix until smooth.

6. Pour batter into springform pan and cover with aluminum foil.

7. Fit pressure cooker with stainless rack and add water.

8. Place springform pan on rack; secure lid.

9. Set pressure cooker to SOUP and timer to 30 minutes.

10. When cooking is complete, remove cheesecake and let cool.

11. Refrigerate for 3 hours before serving.

Deb's Tip:
For a sweeter taste, increase the sugar by a quarter cup.

Coconut Soup

Ingredients:

2 cans (13½ ounces each) light coconut milk

¼ cup small pearl tapioca

¼ cup sugar

¼ cup sweetened coconut, shredded

1 teaspoon coconut extract

1. Place coconut milk, tapioca and sugar into pressure cooker; secure lid.
2. Set pressure cooker to RICE and timer to 6 minutes.
3. When cooking is complete, stir in remaining ingredients; let cool.
4. Pour soup into glasses and serve chilled.

Deb's Tip:
You can find small pearl tapioca in most Asian supermarkets.

Poached Oranges

Ingredients:

4 large navel oranges

1 cup amaretto liqueur

1 cup orange juice

½ cup sugar

1 star anise

1. Place all ingredients into pressure cooker; secure lid.
2. Set pressure cooker to VEGGIE and timer to 5 minutes.
3. When cooking is complete, transfer oranges to a platter.
4. With the lid off, set pressure cooker to VEGGIE and cook until liquid thickens.
5. Remove star anise and pour liquid over oranges.
6. Serve immediately.

Deb's Tip:
Serve this with a piece of coffee cake.

Hot Fudge Cake

Ingredients:

Non-stick cooking spray

2-quart stainless steel bowl or baking insert

1 box (18¼ ounces) chocolate fudge cake mix

1 cup heavy cream

3 large eggs

½ cup unsalted butter

2 cups water

1. Apply non-stick spray to stainless bowl.
2. Place all ingredients, except water, into a food processor; mix until smooth and transfer to stainless bowl.
3. Pour water into pressure cooker and place bowl in water; secure lid.
4. Set pressure cooker to MEAT and timer to 30 minutes.
5. When cooking is complete, invert onto a cake stand and serve.

Dried Fruit Compote

Ingredients:

1 pound dried apricots, cherries or figs
1 cup orange juice
½ cup amaretto liqueur
¼ cup sugar
1 cinnamon stick

1. Place all ingredients into pressure cooker; secure lid.
2. Set pressure cooker to VEGGIE and timer to 5 minutes.
3. When cooking is complete, remove cinnamon stick and serve.

Deb's Tip:
Serve over waffles or French toast.

Easy Flan

Ingredients:

½ cup sugar

1½ cups water, divided

6 custard cups, 4-ounce capacity

1 can (14 ounces) sweetened condensed milk

1 can (12 ounces) evaporated milk

2 large eggs, beaten

2 large egg yolks

1 teaspoon vanilla

1 teaspoon orange zest

1. Preheat stove top on high.
2. In a non-stick pan, combine sugar and ½ cup water; stir until sugar is dissolved.
3. Reduce heat to medium and let sugar mixture cook for several minutes; do not stir.
4. When the water evaporates and the sugar turns to a caramel color, remove from heat and pour caramel into custard cups; let rest for 10 minutes.
5. Pour 1 cup of water into pressure cooker.
6. In a bowl, combine remaining ingredients; stir and pour into custard cups.
7. Cover each cup with aluminum foil and stack cups inside pressure cooker; secure lid.
8. Set pressure cooker to RICE and timer to 6 minutes.
9. When cooking is complete, remove cups and chill until ready to serve.

Bread Pudding

Ingredients:

Non-stick cooking spray

2-quart stainless steel bowl or baking insert

4 cups hard crusted bread, cut into 1-inch cubes

4 large eggs, beaten

1½ cups cream

1½ cups milk

½ cup sugar

1 teaspoon orange zest

1 tablespoon orange flavored liqueur

1 teaspoon vanilla extract

¼ teaspoon salt

½ cup raisins

Aluminum Foil

2 cups water

1. Apply non-stick spray to stainless bowl.
2. Place bread cubes into stainless bowl.
3. In a separate bowl, combine eggs, cream, milk and sugar; mix well.
4. Add zest, liqueur, vanilla and salt to bowl; mix well.
5. Pour egg mixture over bread cubes and add raisins.
6. Cover stainless bowl with aluminum foil.
7. Pour water into pressure cooker and add stainless bowl; secure lid.
8. Set pressure cooker to RICE and timer to 15 minutes.
9. When cooking is complete, serve hot or cold.

Deb's Tip:
The older and harder the bread the better the pudding.

Brandy Poached Pears

Ingredients:

6 firm pears, peeled

3 cups brandy

1 cup sugar

2 cups orange juice

2 star fruits, sliced 1-inch thick

1 cinnamon stick

1. Using a paring knife, cut a small whole in the bottom of each pear and remove the seeds.
2. Cut the bottoms of each pear so they will sit flat.
3. Add remaining ingredients to pressure cooker.
4. Place pears into pressure cooker; secure lid.
5. Set pressure cooker to VEGGIE and timer to 10 minutes.
6. When cooking is complete, gently remove pears and place on a platter.
7. With the lid off, press MEAT again and reduce the liquid for 20 minutes or until thickened.
8. Pour syrup over pears and serve.

wolfgang puck
Bistro
collection
SAFEGUARDS
Bistro
Function
Time
Delay Time
Keep Warm
Cancel

Brown Rice Pudding

Ingredients:

4 cups brown rice, cooked

4 cups milk

⅛ teaspoon salt

½ cup sugar

1 stick cinnamon

½ cup golden raisins

1 tablespoon amaretto liqueur

1. Place all ingredients into pressure cooker; stir and secure lid.
2. Set pressure cooker to RICE and timer to 6 minutes.
3. When cooking is complete, serve immediately.

Blackberry Cream Cheese Coffee Cake

Makes 8 servings

Ingredients:

Non-stick cooking spray

2 cups fresh or frozen blackberries

1 cup sugar

3 teaspoons quick cook tapioca

2 teaspoons orange zest, divided

8 ounces cream cheese, softened

1 box (16 ounces) pound cake mix

¼ cup milk

2 large eggs

1. Apply non-stick spray to pressure cooker.
2. In a bowl, combine blackberries, sugar, tapioca and 1 teaspoon orange zest; transfer to pressure cooker.
3. In a food processor, combine cream cheese, cake mix, milk, eggs and remaining orange zest; mix for 2 minutes or until batter is smooth.
4. Pour batter over blackberries inside the pressure cooker; secure lid.
5. Set pressure cooker to SOUP and timer to 20 minutes.
6. When cooking is complete, let cool for 20 minutes and invert onto a cake stand.
7. Serve warm or cold.

Stuffed Apples

Ingredients:

½ cup brown sugar

3 tablespoons butter, softened

1 teaspoon apple pie spice

4 small apples, cored

1 cinnamon stick

1 cup orange juice

1. In a bowl, combine sugar, butter and apple spice; mix well.
2. Stuff each apple with sugar mixture.
3. Place cinnamon stick and orange juice into pressure cooker.
4. Add apples to pressure cooker and secure lid.
5. Set pressure cooker to VEGGIE and timer to 3 minutes.
6. When cooking is complete, serve immediately.

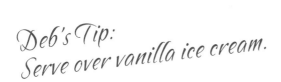
Deb's Tip:
Serve over vanilla ice cream.

Index

Index

Index

Index

Index